The children were at school. They
made a little theatre. They made it
out of a box.

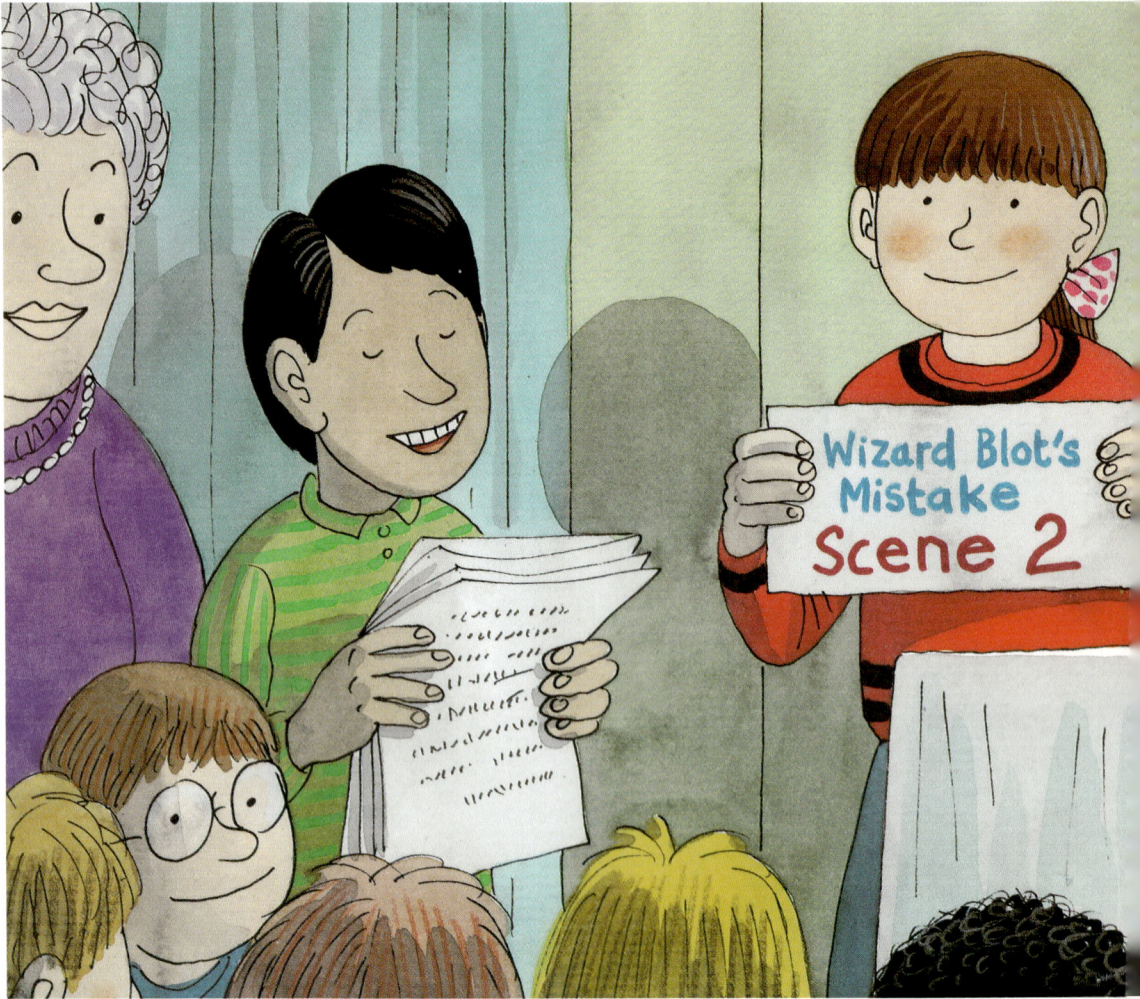

The children put on a play. The play was about a wizard.

He was called Wizard Blot. Wizard
Blot made mistakes.

Wizard Blot made a spell. The spell
went wrong.

"Oh dear! Oh dear!" said Wizard
Blot.

Everyone laughed. Everyone liked the play. Mrs May liked Wizard Blot.

Biff was in her room. The key began
to glow.
"Chip! Chip!" called Biff.

Chip ran into Biff's bedroom. The magic took them inside the little house.

Toma
INDUSTRIES
Wanted
Boy or girl to help. Jobs:
mixing spells
cleaning up
Apply within
BEWARE OF THE DOG

The magic took them to Wizard Blot's house. The Wizard wanted some help.

"Come in!" said the Wizard. "I
wanted one helper, but two will do."

"Come in!" said the Wizard. "You can wash up, then you can tidy up."

Biff and Chip looked at the mess.
"Don't be lazy," said the Wizard, "or
I'll turn you into frogs."

Biff and Chip did the washing up.
"I don't like this," said Chip, "but I
don't want to be a frog."

"I don't like ironing," said Biff, "but we don't want to be frogs."

Oh no! Biff dropped a bottle. It was
vanishing cream.

"Help!" said Biff. "This is vanishing cream."

Chip looked at his hands.
"Oh no," he said. "Bits of us are
vanishing."

He rubbed his face.

"Oh no!" said Biff. "Your face is
vanishing."

"Help! Help!" said the man. "I'm being attacked by the washing."

Wizard Blot came back. Biff told him about the vanishing cream.

Chip gave Wizard Blot the computer
disks. The Wizard was pleased.

It was time to go home.
"Thank you," said Wizard Blot. "Do
come again."

Biff had a little bottle.
"Don't drop it," said Chip. "It's
vanishing cream."